Granddaughters are some of
the sweetest people in the world.
And I'll always be thankful
that the sweetest of all...
turned out to be you.

— Chris Gallatin

There Is Nothing Sweeter in Life Than a Granddaughter

Words to Let a Granddaughter Know How Much She Is Loved

Edited by
Patricia Wayant

Blue Mountain Press™

Boulder, Colorado

Library of Congress Control Number: 2012919508
ISBN: 978-1-59842-706-6

█ and Blue Mountain Press are registered in U.S. Patent and Trademark Office.
Certain trademarks are used under license.

Acknowledgments appear on page 92.

Printed in China.
Eighth Printing: 2017

♻ This book is printed on recycled paper.

This book is printed on paper that has been specially produced to be acid free (neutral pH) and contains no groundwood or unbleached pulp. It conforms with the requirements of the American National Standards Institute, Inc., so as to ensure that this book will last and be enjoyed by future generations.

Blue Mountain Arts, Inc.

P.O. Box 4549, Boulder, Colorado 80306

Contents

(Authors listed in order of first appearance)

To My Sweet Granddaughter

A granddaughter is one
of life's greatest treasures,
and there is nothing
sweeter in life.

The day you came into my world,
my life changed forever.
You are someone I can spoil
and love unconditionally.

My heart is filled with pride
as I see all the amazing
    things you do.
You remind me of all
    that is fun in life
and make me smile
each time I think of you.
I cherish the times
    we spend together
because these are some
of the happiest days of my life.
Thank you for sharing
so much of your life with me.

— Peggy Wharton-Goroly

I Hope You Know
How Much
You Are Loved

You may not understand
just how much your life means
to those around you —
how our days are brighter
    because you're here
and how the sound of your laughter
touches the hearts of everyone
    around you.

Your presence adds something special
    and invaluable to the world.
You bring joy to those who love you
    and a smile to everyone you meet.

Though you may not realize it,
your life is a gift that
is treasured.
With each new day, I hope
you will know how much
you are loved.

— Star Nakamoto

What a Difference You Make in My Life!

You give me plenty
of reasons to smile.
Every day is special with you in it.
I want you to know how proud I am
to be your grandparent
and how proud I am of you too.
You are a wonderful person
and a beautiful reminder
of all the joy I've known
since you were born.

You always amaze me
with your charm
and your sweet self…
you are precious in every way.
I'll always cherish the
time we share.
I wish you happiness,
love, laughter,
and a lifetime of
dreams come true.

— Dianne Cogar

I Wish I Could Do All These Things for You

I wish I could make sure
    you always had the best —
like laughter, rainbows,
    butterflies, and health.
I wish I could take you anywhere
    you wanted to go
and treat you to waterfalls,
    rivers, forests, and mountaintops.
I wish I could make it possible for you
to do anything you ever dreamed of,
even if just for a day.
I wish I could keep you from
    ever being hurt or sad
and that all your troubles
    and problems would disappear.
I wish I could package up
all the memories that bring smiles to you
and have them handy for
    your immediate enjoyment.

I wish I could guarantee
you peace of mind, contentment,
    faith, and strength,
as well as the constant ability
    to find joy in all the things
that sometimes go unnoticed.
I wish you could always have
moments to connect
    with other individuals
who are full of smiles and
    hugs to give away
and stories and laughter to share.
I wish you could always know
    how much you mean to me.

— Barbara Cage

"Special"
Is the Word That
Best Describes You...

"Special" is a word that is used
to describe something
    one of a kind,
like a hug or a sunset
or a person who spreads love
with a smile or kind gesture.

"Special" describes people
who act from the heart
and keep in mind the hearts
    of others.

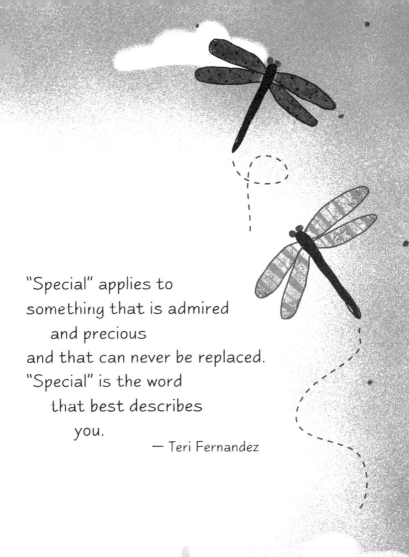

"Special" applies to
something that is admired
and precious
and that can never be replaced.
"Special" is the word
that best describes
you.

— Teri Fernandez

You Are
the World's Greatest
Granddaughter

You have a way about you
that brings a smile to my lips
and happiness to my heart.
The way your eyes shine
lights up my entire being,
and the sound of your voice
touches my soul.
Whether we are near or apart,
I am always filled
with your delightful spirit.
I am grateful for the joy
you have brought to my life
and for the love we share.

— Susan Wigden

Watching you grow up
and spending time with you
is a part of my life
I wouldn't trade for the world.
You are just that important to me.
A granddaughter like you
makes the world a happy place.
My life is so worthwhile and exciting
just by having you in it!

— Dianne Cogar

There's Only One You

There is only one of you.
Don't ever compare yourself
   to anyone,
because no one else will ever shine
in quite the same way you do.
You are wonderfully special
just as you are.

Every hair on your head is precious
and every creative thought you have
is priceless.
You add so much to this world already,
and you're just getting started.
I am really proud of how you treat others.
You are thoughtful and polite,
and it's easy to forget to act that way.
Thank you for remembering.

And thanks for being one-of-a-kind,
spectacular, world-brightening...
you!

— Amy Kuo

It seems that no matter what you undertake in life, you do so with a joyful and positive attitude. You work hard and try your best, pouring your heart into all you do. You demonstrate sincere gratitude and don't take your loved ones for granted. You never just "follow the crowd," and I admire the firm stand you take in maintaining your individuality.

— Debbie Burton-Peddle

You never give in. You never give up.
You believe in yourself. You have
learned to trust your own capabilities.
And I'm here to tell you... that might
very well be the most important thing
you ever learn. Hold tight to that
confidence and to all you've discovered,
as you set out on the road to your
dreams. Get ready to meet your
own greatness.
— Charley Knox

The Absolutely True Story of an Amazing Girl... You!

Once there was a girl… and she was unique and talented and interesting and amazing and unforgettable… and real. And she knew, deep down, that if she tried something and things didn't go as she had hoped or wanted or dreamed or planned, she could just try something different or try the exact same thing again but approach it in a new or different way. Then, one day, her greatest hopes and dreams actually became true.

And so her life was full of all these
amazing and unforgettable moments and
events and circumstances: incredible wins,
of course, but also equally incredible — and
worth it — losses. Because no matter what
happened, she learned from everything around
her and everything she went through. Yes,
she fell sometimes (like everybody else does),
but she got up and moved forward by always
being true to herself. And maybe one day
she will even make a path for others to follow...
until they can make their own paths too.

You see, it's not that she was never
frightened or sad or even knew when she
woke up each day what to do (no one does).
It was simply that she believed in herself
and always shined on like a star. Just like you.

— Ashley Rice

You Have So Many Wonderful Gifts

I see your gifts reflected in others.
I watch them savor your smiling eyes.
I watch them brighten up
when you shower them
with your spontaneous laughter.
I watch them when you look
into their eyes and ask them
how they are doing —
they can tell you really want to know.
These are the moments they remember
at the end of their day.

You have the gift of giving
and the gift of receiving.
You accept the quiet "thank you"
whispered in gratitude,
the glimpse of a happy tear,
and the face beaming love back to you.
You allow them to slip into your heart
and energize your soul.
You return that love to them joyfully.

You make a difference in others' lives,
and you allow them to make
a difference in yours.

— Susan L. Roberts

When I Look at You, Granddaughter...

I see an amazing,
one-of-a-kind individual
with unique talents and abilities —
someone who deserves all the joy,
happiness, and abundance
you can imagine.
You've been blessed
in so many ways,
but I know sometimes
it can be hard to see that
when you're caught up
in all the challenges of life.

For those times when you
might not be able to see for yourself
how very special you are,
please read these words.
Let them be a reminder
that you are precious to me.
You are an amazing,
exceptional, and worthy person
with more to offer than you know.
You have touched my life
and so many others,
and you have made
this world a better place
just because you are in it.

— Jason Blume

You Are Everything a Granddaughter Should Be

A granddaughter is memories
that take us by surprise,
a shining glimpse of tomorrow
wrapped in cuddles and smiles.
A granddaughter is lullabies
and music for your soul —
a song that makes you feel
so much richer
just for having heard it.
A granddaughter is fun —
a bit of stardust in your hand
and all the things money cannot buy.

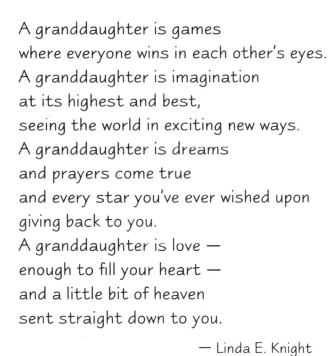

A granddaughter is games
where everyone wins in each other's eyes.
A granddaughter is imagination
at its highest and best,
seeing the world in exciting new ways.
A granddaughter is dreams
and prayers come true
and every star you've ever wished upon
giving back to you.
A granddaughter is love —
enough to fill your heart —
and a little bit of heaven
sent straight down to you.

— Linda E. Knight

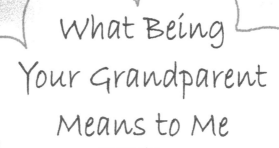

What Being Your Grandparent Means to Me

Being your grandparent means that I have had the opportunity to experience loving someone more than I love myself. I have learned what it's like to experience joy and pain through someone else's life.

It has brought me pride and joy; your accomplishments touch me and thrill me like no one else's can. It has brought me a few tears and heartaches on your behalf, but it has taught me hope and patience. It has shown me the depth, strength, and power of love.

No one has ever made me as satisfied as you do just by being happy. No one has made me as proud as you do just by living up to your responsibilities. No one's smile has ever warmed my heart like yours does; no one's laughter fills my heart with delight as quickly as yours can. No one's hugs feel as sweet, and no one's dreams mean as much to me as yours do.

No other memories are as rewarding as those we share, where lessons were learned and humorous stories abound; where the good times have become precious treasures to relive again and again.

You are a part of me, and I will always accept, appreciate, adore, and love you unconditionally. Being your grandparent means that I've been given one of life's greatest gifts: you.

— Barbara Cage

Some Wonderful Wisdom I'd Like to Share with You

Girls rule! ❀ You can do anything ❀ Learn from the amazing women around you ❀ Play with wild abandon ❀ Learn to dream with your eyes wide open ❀ Think big… if that doesn't work, think bigger ❀ Life is all about how you handle Plan B — it's the true test of character ❀ Your future does not lie in front of you; it resides deep inside you ❀

Forgive everyone everything ❀ Play fair, even when others don't ❀ Honor your legacy with your integrity ❀ No one can make you feel inferior unless you give them permission to do so ❀ There's no right way to do a wrong thing ❀ Rise by lifting others ❀ In the end, good girls always win ❀ Never forget that I will love you forever, for always, and no matter what ❀ You tolerate my hugs and kisses, and you keep me young at heart ❀ You are absolutely over-the-top amazing... don't ever forget it! ❀

— Suzy Toronto

Always Remember Who You Are...

Remember where you came from
    and where you've been.
Remember that nothing can destroy you.
Life can only make you bigger, better,
and brighter... if you allow it to do so.
Remember to always help light the
    way for others.
Think of it not as your work or even
    your purpose but as your destiny.
You are empowering and brilliant,
    creative and inspiring.
Remember this always
    as you continue being you.

— Jane Almarie Lewis

There is no one in the past, present,
or future who will ever offer the world what
you do. No one will think, act, or smile
exactly like you. No one will be able to come
up with your unique points of view.

Don't hold back who you really are. When you
are true to yourself, you glow. When you are
passionate about your dreams, you shine.
When you live fully, people are drawn to you —
people who love you for just being you.

— April Aragam

Believe in Yourself and All You Want to Be

Don't let what other people say or do make you frown. Laugh as much as possible. Let in the good times and get through the bad. Be happy with who and where you are. You are in the right place, and your heart is leading you on the way to a great tomorrow. When circumstances seem difficult, pull through them. This will make you stronger than you think.

The longer you practice the habit
of working toward your dreams,
the easier the journey will become.

You were meant for great things.
Learn as much as possible. Always
follow your dreams.

— Ashley Rice

You're on the Journey of a Lifetime...

A journey no one else will travel and no one else can judge — a path of happiness and hurt, where the challenges are great and the rewards even greater. You're on a journey where each experience will teach you something valuable and you can't get lost, for you already know the way by heart.

You're on a journey that is universal yet uniquely personal, and profound yet astonishingly simple — where sometimes you will stumble and other times you will soar. You'll learn that even at your darkest point you can find a light — if you look for it. At the most difficult crossroad, you'll have an answer — if you listen for it.

Friends and family will accompany you part of the way, and you'll walk the rest by yourself... but you will never be alone. Travel at your own pace. There'll be time enough to learn all you need to know and go as far as you're meant to go. Travel light. Letting go of extra baggage will keep your arms open and your heart free to fully embrace the gifts of the moment.

You may not always know exactly where you're headed, but if you follow the desires of your heart, the integrity of your conscience, and the wisdom of your soul... then each step you take will lead you to discover more of who you really are, and it will be a step in the right direction on the journey of a lifetime.

— Paula Finn

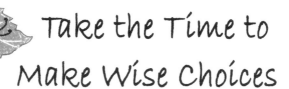

Take the Time to Make Wise Choices

Decisions are incredibly important things! Good decisions will come back to bless you. Bad decisions can come back to haunt you.

That's why it's so important that you take the time to choose wisely...

Choose to do the things that will reflect well... on your ability, your integrity, your spirit, your health, your tomorrows, your smiles, your dreams, and yourself.

You are such a wonder. You're the only one in the universe exactly like you! I want you to take care of that rare and remarkable soul.

I want you to know that there is someone who will thank you for doing the things you do now with foresight and wisdom and respect.

It's the person you will someday be.

You have a chance to make that person so thankful and so proud. All you have to do is remember one of the lessons I learned when I made a similar journey. It's pretty simple, really, just these nine little words:

Each time you come to a crossroads ...choose wisely.
— Douglas Pagels

Remember What Is Most Important...

It's not having everything go right;
it's facing whatever goes wrong.
It's not being without fear;
it's having the determination
    to go on in spite of it.
It's not where you stand,
but the direction you're going in.
It's more than never
    having bad moments;
it's knowing you are always
    bigger than the moment.

It's believing you have already
      been given everything
you need to handle life.
It's not being able to rid
      the world of all its injustices;
it's being able to rise above them.
It's the belief in your heart
      that there will always be
more good than bad in the world.

Remember to live just this one day
and not add tomorrow's troubles
      to today's load.
Remember that every day ends
and brings a new tomorrow
full of exciting new things.
Love what you do,
      do the best you can,
and always remember
      how much you are loved.

— Vickie M. Worsham

Don't Ever Lose Faith in Yourself

In those times when
you may feel a little uncertain
about your future,
you need to trust your
decisions and feelings
and do what is best for you.
The future will work itself out;
you're the kind of person
who can make it happen.
Don't let anyone else's negativity
influence your dreams, values, or hopes.
Focus on what you can change
and let go of what you can't.
You know your own worth,
what you've accomplished,
and what you're capable of.

Your goals may take a bit longer
and be harder to achieve
than you had hoped,
but concentrate on the positives
and combine faith with
generous portions of patience
and determination.
Step boldly and confidently
    into your future
where happiness, success,
and dreams await you.

You have the potential
    for greatness...
never give up.
                — Barbara Cage

You Are a Bright and Shining Star

Sometimes the hardest times in our lives are what push us further, inspire us to be bolder, teach us about real hope, dreams, and how to believe… They help us to become the greatest version of that person we always hoped we'd be.

I'm proud of all you've achieved and
everything you are. No matter what
circumstance, state, or place you
may find yourself in some days, just
keep being you: a bold, bright star.

— Ashley Rice

I remember watching you
take your first unsteady steps,
your legs wobbly and unsure.
I wanted to catch you,
protect you, and keep you safe,
but soon your steps became steadier,
and you ran farther and farther from me.
I loved watching you grow
more independent and mature
even as you became
more separate and individual.
Now I watch you take
your first steps into the world.
A more vast and rich tapestry awaits you
than the carpets of our family room
and the tiles of our kitchen floor.

Though I still want
to pull you to me to keep you safe,
I want you to know I am so proud
of the tremendous person you have become.
You have my love,
my pride, and my respect.
As I watch you venture out into
this new, exciting stage of life,
I know your steps
will become sure-footed,
and soon you will be
running once more toward
the infinite possibilities
you can dream for yourself.

— Jessica Dainty Johns

There's Nothing You Can't Do

Believe in yourself
as I believe in you.
Trust in your strengths
as I trust in them.

Look in the mirror
and see what I see —
a talented, uplifting,
and magnificent person
who can do anything
and everything she wants.

Believe in your heart
that you have the power
to grab hold of your future
and mold it into the things
you have always dreamed of.

Trust in your soul
that you are capable of doing
all that needs to be done.

Know that you are
incredible in every way,
and see yourself
as others see you…
as an intelligent
and spectacular person.

— Lamisha Serf

You See...

You see a girl
but I see a doctor
who could one day find the cure

A teacher
whose words are like gold
to all those she teaches

I see a scientist
who will discover
things we never knew existed

A model
whose face will change the
way girls see themselves

You see a girl
but I see something extraordinary
amazing and original

You see a girl
but I see the next face
on a football magazine

The first female president
of the U.S.A. taking charge

I see someone who will unlock hidden
secrets and many closed doors

You see a girl with no hope, no dreams
and what seems to be no future

But I see a girl with the biggest imagination
just bursting to be set free

You see a girl
I see a dream
                    — Hannah Poe

My Granddaughter Is a Genius

When my granddaughter surprises me
by saying "please" and "thank you"
it seems that this is normal
for a three-year-old

When my granddaughter amazes me
by offering me her cookie
it seems that all three-year-olds do that too

When my granddaughter sings a song
almost right on tune
no one seems to find it extraordinary

When my granddaughter twirls around
in rhythm to the music
no one stops to watch her
with much admiration

Except her grandmother

— Natasha Josefowitz

There is an ineffable bond between this granddaughter and me. I felt it the first moment I held her, minutes after she was born. I love her spirit and her stubborn brilliance. The kid is a character, a big personality with a crackly voice and an accent that makes her sound like a miniature Brooklyn dock worker. She is simply irresistible to me. When she was two days old, an astrologer told me that the position of the planets and stars at the moment of her birth ensured that she'd be a spitfire. Some people who know us both say she reminds them of me.

I would dive into a burning building for this girl.

— Barbara Graham

A Special Night

When my granddaughter, Rebekah, was in the sixth grade, her school had a Valentine's father/daughter banquet and dance. Unfortunately, her father, who is my son, had to be out of town on business, so Rebekah invited me to escort her to the banquet. It was an unforgettable evening for both of us. I will always remember how much I enjoyed the evening and how very proud I was to have been invited by Rebekah. There were many men and boys she could have invited to go in her father's place, but she chose me! I wrote the following poem, "First Dance," to commemorate this, her first dance. (We were both pleased at how well we did on the dance floor.)

First Dance

Body and spirit dancing and whirling,
Head to toe sliding and twirling,
Into his arms, then onto her toes,
While in her veins excitement flows.
Eyes flashing and heart set awhirl;
This beautiful young dancing girl
Glides to the music's rhythmic beat;
Her smile tender, happy, and sweet.

On the dance floor gliding and shifting;
His leaden feet moving and lifting,
His old body wearying and tiring,
Yet, his heart for more was crying.
Days of his youth now returning,
For more energy he was yearning.
With love and pride his heart was growing;
His eyes and smiles sparkling and glowing.

For them, this was their first dance.
He was there only by chance.
He, her old loving granddad
Whose heart she had made so glad.
She, loving granddaughter, young and bright,
Had invited him to the dance that night,
Where precious memories none can sever
Were etched into their hearts forever.

— Royce W. Wilkerson

Granddaughter, You Make Every Day Beautiful for Me

Every day, I think about you —
and the feelings that come shining through
are the most beautiful kind.
Each day, I think about you —
and our times together blossom in my mind.
I'm glad I have your hand to hold,
and your kind, generous heart
to give me all the things money can't buy.
I have your smiles to remind me
how important we are to each other's life.

Each thought of you
makes the most beautiful bouquet.
I hope that each time
you think of me,
you will see all the smiles
I have just for you,
my gratitude to you for being
such a loving granddaughter,
and all the love for you
that shines from my heart.

— Jacqueline Schiff

Why God Made Little Girls

God made the world with the towering trees
Majestic mountains and restless seas
Then paused and said, "It needs one more thing —
Someone to laugh and dance and sing —
To walk in the woods and gather flowers —
To commune with nature in quiet hours."
So God made little girls
With laughing eyes and bouncing curls —
With joyful hearts and infectious smiles —
Enchanting ways and feminine wiles —
And when He completed the task He'd begun,
He was pleased and proud of the job He'd done;
For the world, when seen through a little girl's eyes
Greatly resembles paradise.

— Author Unknown

Child of my child,
Heart of my heart.
Your smile bridges
The years between us...
I am young again, discovering
The world through your eyes.
You have the time to listen
And I have the time to spend,
Delighted to gaze at familiar,
Loved features made new in you again.
Through you, I see the future.
Through me, you'll see the past.
In the present, we'll love one another
As long as these moments last.

— Author Unknown

Family Is the Best Feeling in the World

The best feeling in this world
   is family.
From it, we draw love,
   friendship, moral support,
and the fulfillment of every
   special need within our hearts.

In a family, we are connected to
   an ever-present source
of sunny moments, smiles and laughter,
understanding and encouragement,
and hugs that help us grow in confidence
   all along life's path.

Wherever we are,
whatever we're doing,
whenever we really need to feel especially
loved, befriended, supported,
 and cared for in the greatest way,
our hearts can turn to family
and find the very best
  always waiting for us.

     — Barbara J. Hall

Because We're Family...

Because we're family, you will always
have a place to go where arms are open
and hearts want to know what they can
do to keep you happy, healthy, and safe.

Because we're family, you have a haven
where you can laugh and play and renew the
energies exhausted by stress and strain —
a sanctuary where you can heal from pain
and sorrow and find hope and faith.

There's understanding that comes from
years of knowing each other — and empathy
and compassion from people who care.

Because we're family, you have customs
and traditions to keep with the people
who are linked to you in history and
in the precious memories we've built
together. You are drawn to the family
circle with warmth and shining smiles.

You have a snug spot where you are
always comfortable — and loved ones
are gathered around to love, support,
and rejoice in the highlights of your life.

— Jacqueline Schiff

To You, Granddaughter, I Give...

My time when you need someone
to listen or stand with you.
My heart when you need
someone to care.
My support when you need to know
what a great person you are.
My faith in you,
in your goals and dreams,
and in your ability to achieve them.
My perspective for when you are
confused and want another opinion.

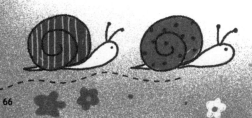

My strength for when the path
you walk seems all uphill
and you need to rest a bit.
My understanding when you make
mistakes or don't live up
to your own expectations
and you need to know that
you don't have to be perfect.

Most of all,
I give you my heart always,
for the bond between us
is unconditional.
— Ruthann Tholen

Remember That You Can Always Count on Me

When life isn't easy and you wonder if anyone understands what you're going through, I want you to reach out to me. Even if we find ourselves miles apart, don't ever forget that my heart is filled with so many hopes for your happiness.

I want you to feel like you can tell me everything that's on your mind. I want to be able to help you find a million more smiles and make your days more joyful and filled with all the serenity you so dearly deserve.

When you wonder if there is anyone who
cares completely and unconditionally,
look my way. Let down your guard,
and know that it's okay to bare your
soul with someone who knows you
as well as I do. When you need to
talk things out, realize that you'll
find a very loving listener... in me.

It doesn't matter what it's for; if it's
important to you, then it's important
to me. What matters most is that
you gently remember: sometimes two
heads (and two hearts) are better
than one can be, and you can always
count on me to be there for you.

— Douglas Pagels

I Want to Thank You

I was so beautifully blessed to have been given the gift of a granddaughter like you.

Our special connection means more to me with the passing of every season. We have a bond that just keeps blossoming… and a love we can count on to never go away.

There are times when my eyes fill up with tears just from thinking of how dear you are. But there are many more times when my heart fills up with smiles just from knowing how close and caring we'll always be.

— Kelly Lise

The gifts you give everyone all through the year — the ones that come from your kind and caring heart — are priceless. Thank you for so many big things — and a million little things — that help bring happiness into other people's lives.

You are such a joy to everyone who is fortunate enough to know you!

And I am so glad that I've had the privilege of being one of those lucky people.

— Terry Bairnson

You Are a Dream Come True

Granddaughter, you have made the sunlight shine in my life more than you will ever know, and you have filled me with so much pride! It's really hard to keep all that admiration and love inside, and you'll have to forgive me for bragging about you to anyone who will take the time to listen.

The many photographs I have of you fill my house in the same way that all my precious memories of you fill my heart — with a deep and lasting happiness.

Of all the dreams I've had in my life — the ones of being a parent and a grandparent, of sharing such a sweet family love, and of having so many happy wishes come true — one of the very best things has been watching a miracle in the making.

Because that lovely miracle… is you.

— Laurel Atherton

I Couldn't Be More Proud of You

The day you were born, I remember feeling something I had never felt before. Looking at you — so small and innocent — I realized to myself I was now officially a "grandparent."

Though I wouldn't take you home and raise you, I could love you, spoil you, and enjoy you. Being your grandparent became one of my favorite things to do.

I realize how much joy and happiness you have brought to my life and how much better my world is because you're a part of it. I look forward to watching you grow even more and sharing with you all the great things that will come your way. I hope you'll always remember how important you are to me, how much I love you, and how very proud I am to be your grandparent.

— Debra Heintz Cavataio

It Seems like Only Yesterday...

Where did the time go?
It seems like only yesterday
you snuggled in my arms minutes
    after you were born.
A dainty little hand with five tiny fingers
    grasping mine.
It seems like only yesterday I saw you go
from a crawl to a walk to running like a deer —
from throwing toys to throwing balls through hoops.
It seems like just last weekend you came for
    one of many sleepovers.
We had a sock fight, laughed till our stomachs hurt,
    went to the movies, played games,
        and took the dog for a walk.
It seems like only yesterday that I went
    to your first dance recital
where I sat peering through the heads in front
    of me to catch a glimpse of you onstage.
You were easy to find because, after all,
    you were the cutest and the best.

So many things, too many to count,
    happened only yesterday.
Now our times together have become
    fewer and farther between.
But you are well and happy, enjoying life,
    and doing what kids do,
and for that I'm grateful.
I thank God for bringing you into my life,
and I thank you for bringing me more joy
    than I could ever imagine.
I'm so proud of the young woman you're becoming.
I'm proud of your mother and father for the way
    they have raised you.
I only pray that somehow in those fleeting,
    quality moments we got to share
that I added as much to your life
        as you have to mine.

                — Joan C. Monahan

You Continue to Amaze Me

Each year you grow stronger and more confident in who you are, setting new goals and challenges. You are rich in talent and ambition, shining in every endeavor you embark upon. You extend your generosity and kindness to everyone you encounter, spreading such positive energy through your gentle actions.

All this has created the amazing person you have always been and will continue to be.

— Jeanmarie A. Swiontkowski

You are bright, talented, and creative.
You have a spirit of adventure and an
intense desire to make the world better.
You are sensitive to the needs of others
and passionate about helping people.
You are driven to reach dreams that
will make your future so much brighter.
You have an inner spark that kindles
a light in everyone your life touches.

You are a precious gift
to the present and the future,
and you must never forget this.

— Jacqueline Schiff

The Future Is Yours

I feel overwhelmed with joy when I think of all that awaits you. It's a big, beautiful world out there, with so much to see and do. I hope you find that all of God's amazing creations astound you as much as they do me. And I hope you go through life with so much love in your heart that it makes you long to live life to the absolute fullest.

I hope your life is filled with so many new discoveries and your heart with the desires to seek them. I also hope that some part of me will be with you to share in your happiness along the way.

I hope you take into all your tomorrows my everlasting love and wisdom. Though we have only experienced a small amount of the wonders of the world together, we have shared a bountiful love between us. The memories we've made are buried deep in my heart for safekeeping.

As you go into the future, I pray that you love just as much as you live. I hope you will mold your life into something very special and rewarding — something you will someday long to share with a granddaughter of your own.

— Dianne Cogar

It's a Blessing and a Privilege to Be Your Grandparent

The things we share are so special to me;
I'll cherish them for a lifetime.
Spending time with you is something
I've always looked forward to
ever since you were a baby.

You've added so much joy to my life.
Though we come from different generations,
our hearts share the same laughter
and the same love.
Those are two things in life
that age cannot change.

If I could tell you a million times a day
that I love you — and hug you just as much —
that still would never be enough
to express just how much you mean to me.
I hope you are reminded of my love for you
in some small ways throughout your life.

My love is a legacy I leave to you.
I want you to know I wish
the very best for you always.
Being a part of your life is
a blessing and a privilege.

— Dianne Cogar

My Many Wishes for You

I want you to always be safe and secure. I want you to be well and at peace with yourself. I want you to get from life all that you desire and more. I want you to feel free to do whatever you want and to let that freedom soar. I want you to know love and be surrounded by it, to bear no pain and feel no hurt.

I want you to be the best person you can be. I want you to share the wonderful gift of yourself with others — how very lucky are those who will receive that beauty!

— Debbie Burton-Peddle

I wish you a heart that's filled with
    friendship and love.
Memories you'll treasure forever.
Faith and courage... to rise above.
And reminders of how special you are.

I wish you joy... to give you twinkles
    in your eyes.
Blessings from angels in disguise.
Health and hope on this
    journey through life.
And the very best of everything!

— Douglas Pagels

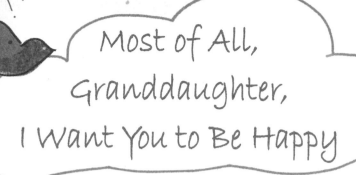

Most of All, Granddaughter, I Want You to Be Happy

Chase your wishes and follow
   your dreams.
Carry the sun inside you.
Get a little closer, every single day,
   to the hopes that you want
      to come true.
Reach for your stars, brighten
   your days.
Fill your heart in a thousand ways.
Be happy, Granddaughter.

I love you so much, and I wish you
    such wonderful things.
I wish you joys only a dreamer
    would dream
and things only a grandparent
    would wish for.
And this I will always pray:

May you never forget
    that my heart and my hopes
        are with you
            each step of the way.

— Laurel Atherton

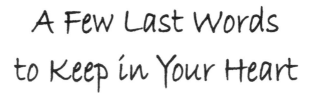

A Few Last Words to Keep in Your Heart

If a star twinkles... wish on it. When you spot a rainbow... search for the gold. Walk on the sunny side; dream on a cloud. Always remember that life is meant to be enjoyed.

Be gracious... angels are watching. Unfold your wings; rise and soar. Fill your life with wonder and your days with beauty. Set your dreams on the farthest star. When you're caught between a rock and a hard place... plant a seed. Chart your course; map out your future. Sail away on your own cruise line, and remember there's no limit to how far you can go.

Believe in miracles. Look for silver linings. When the going gets tough... let faith smooth the way. Dreams come in all shapes and sizes. Do the things that warm your soul. Inspire yourself. Make good things happen. In every tomorrow a new promise shines.

Believe in yourself. Honor your strengths. A little hope and determination can overcome anything. Life is a candle... and you're its spark. Soar high and far. Open your arms and let life's good things come in. God has some spectacular moments designed for you — and no one is more deserving than you.

Live your wishes. Blaze your own trail straight to the stars. Wherever you go... take a prayer with you. Follow your vision wherever it leads. Life is a gift and so are you. Wisdom, love, dreams, and angels... may all these walk with you in the years to come.

— Linda E. Knight

Granddaughter, I Love You So Much

The day you were born,
this world became a better place.
Your smile lights up so many hearts,
your kindness touches so many lives,
and your willingness
to give so much of yourself
    has made a real difference.

What I want to give you
is the knowledge that you truly are
a gift to those around you.

I want to fill your heart
with the peace, joy, and satisfaction
that come from knowing
you mean so much to so many people.

I want you to know you are
appreciated, loved,
and cherished.

— Jason Blume

Acknowledgments

We gratefully acknowledge the permission granted by the following authors, publishers, and authors' representatives to reprint poems or excerpts from their publications.

Peggy Wharton-Goroly for "To My Sweet Granddaughter." Copyright © 2013 by Peggy Wharton-Goroly. All rights reserved.

Susan Wigden for "You Are the World's Greatest Granddaughter." Copyright © 2013 by Susan Wigden. All rights reserved.

Dianne Cogar for "Watching you grow up...," "The Future Is Yours," and "It's a Blessing and a Privilege...." Copyright © 2013 by Dianne Cogar. All rights reserved.

Jason Blume for "When I Look at You, Granddaughter..." and "Granddaughter, I Love You So Much." Copyright © 2011, 2012 by Jason Blume. All rights reserved.

Linda E. Knight for "You Are Everything a Granddaughter Should Be" and "A Few Last Words to Keep in Your Heart." Copyright © 2013 by Linda E. Knight. All rights reserved.

Suzy Toronto for "Some Wonderful Wisdom I'd Like to Share with You." Copyright © 2013 by Suzy Toronto. All rights reserved.

April Aragam for "There is no one in the past...." Copyright © 2013 by April Aragam. All rights reserved.

Hannah Poe for "You See...." Copyright © 2013 by Hannah Poe. All rights reserved.

Natasha Josefowitz for "My Granddaughter Is a Genius" from TOO WISE TO WANT TO BE YOUNG AGAIN. Copyright © 1995 by Natasha Josefowitz. All rights reserved.

HarperCollins Publishers for "There is an ineffable bond between..." from EYE OF MY HEART: 27 WRITERS REVEAL THE HIDDEN PLEASURES AND PERILS OF BEING A GRANDMOTHER by Barbara Graham. Copyright © 2009 by Barbara Graham. All rights reserved.

Royce W. Wilkerson for "A Special Night" from SENSE AND NONSENSE: A COLLECTION OF POEMS AND STORIES IN PROSE AND VERSE. Copyright © 2012 by Royce W. Wilkerson. All rights reserved.

Jacqueline Schiff for "Granddaughter, You Make Every Day Beautiful for Me." Copyright © 2013 by Jacqueline Schiff. All rights reserved.

Debra Heintz Cavataio for "I Couldn't Be More Proud of You." Copyright © 2013 by Debra Heintz Cavataio. All rights reserved.

Joan C. Monahan for "It Seems like Only Yesterday...." Copyright © 2013 by Joan C. Monahan. All rights reserved.

A careful effort has been made to trace the ownership of selections used in this anthology in order to obtain permission to reprint copyrighted material and give proper credit to the copyright owners. If any error or omission has occurred, it is completely inadvertent, and we would like to make corrections in future editions provided that written notification is made to the publisher:

BLUE MOUNTAIN ARTS, INC., P.O. Box 4549, Boulder, Colorado 80306.